LANCASHIRE'S LAST DAYS OF S'

by
Tom Heavyside

Basking in the afternoon sunshine at Patricroft shed at Eccles, west of Manchester, on 6 April 1968 were two 4-6-0s, BR Standard class 5 No. 73050 and 'Black 5' No. 45392. The depot code for Patricroft (9H) had been hand-painted rather prominently on the smokebox door of No. 73050 in place of the former cast-metal plate which denoted this detail. The less-obvious 9F applied to the front of No. 45392 indicated it was allocated to Heaton Mersey shed. Patricroft shed, one of the last half-dozen to operate steam on BR, closed on 1 July 1968. Shortly afterwards No. 73050 was bought for preservation and is now based on the Nene Valley Railway near Peterborough.

Text and photographs © Tom Heavyside, 2004.
First published in the United Kingdom, 2004,
by Stenlake Publishing,
Telephone 01290 551122
Printed by Cordfall Ltd, G21 2QA

ISBN 1 84033 285 9

The publishers regret that they cannot supply
copies of any pictures featured in this book.

ACKNOWLEDGEMENTS

I would like to place on record my sincere thanks to Paul Abell, John Burnett, John Fozard and Ron Herbert for their ready help in the completion of this volume.

Principal workhorses in Lancashire during the last days of steam were the Stanier 'Black 5' 4-6-0s. They handled a wide range of duties including the final steam passenger turns, among them the 'Belfast Boat Express' between Manchester Victoria and Heysham Harbour, the last titled train on BR to be hauled by steam, and which finally succumbed to diesel haulage from 6 May 1968. The first of the class off the production lines was actually manufactured in Lancashire, No. (4)5020 leaving Vulcan Foundry at Newton-le-Willows in August 1934, six months before No. (4)5000 emerged from Crewe Works. In all 842 were built, the last one, No. 44687, also in Lancashire at Horwich Works, near Bolton, in May 1951. In September 1950 the Lancashire sheds had charge of 205 'Black 5s', a total that had increased to 234 by April 1965, and it was not until 1967 that their numbers started to decline. Here, No. 44675, released into traffic from Horwich in March 1950, heads a passenger train bound for Manchester up the West Coast Main Line past Skew Bridge signal box, south of Preston, on 2 September 1967. The post on the left indicates a distance of 20½ miles from Parkside, on the original route from Euston to the north via Earlestown.

INTRODUCTION

Prior to local government reorganisation in 1974, the County Palatine of Lancaster extended from the River Mersey, which marked the boundary in the south, to Hawkshead and Coniston in the north (in what is now part of Cumbria), and from the Irish Sea coast in the west to the foothills of the Pennines in the east. In steam days it was a region of marked contrasts, ranging from the densely populated, heavily industrialised areas of south and east Lancashire to the undoubted grandeur and delights of the Lake District.

Although by no means the first railway, arguably the George Stephenson-engineered Liverpool & Manchester Railway, which opened in September 1830, was the catalyst for the expansion of the railway system not just within Lancashire but, indeed, throughout the United Kingdom. As far as Lancashire is concerned, by the end of the Victorian era a complex web of rails had been laid across the whole county, with a number of companies being responsible for their construction.

However, at the start of the twentieth century, due to various amalgamations, the Lancashire & Yorkshire Railway (L&YR) and the London & North Western Railway (LNWR) had emerged as the two most prominent companies in Lancashire. In addition, the Cheshire Lines Committee, a joint concern formed by the Great Central, Great Northern and Midland railways, was competing for a share of the lucrative traffic on offer between Manchester and Liverpool by means of its line via Warrington Central. The CLC also operated the Southport & Cheshire Lines Extension Railway which ran north from Aintree to Southport Lord Street, while the Great Central served Wigan and St Helens in its own right by way of a connection with the CLC at Glazebrook. Further, both the Midland and Great Central railways had separate interests in the Manchester area, with the Great Western Railway also having access to this important city by way of running powers along the LNWR-owned tracks between Warrington Bank Quay and Manchester Exchange. In the north the Midland Railway owned the line to Lancaster and Morecambe from Settle Junction, while west of Carnforth, to the north of Morecambe Bay, the Furness Railway held sway.

In 1923, when Britain's railways were grouped into four major companies, most of the system within Lancashire was taken over by the London Midland & Scottish Railway (LMS), although the assets of the former Great Central Railway passed to the London & North Eastern Railway (LNER). At the same time the property of the Cheshire Lines Committee was vested jointly in the LMS and the LNER, the latter, which acquired two-thirds of the shares, then becoming responsible for providing the motive power, just as the Great Central had been in earlier years. Similarly, in January 1948, when the railways were nationalised, while most of the county's lines became part of British Railways London Midland Region, the former LNER interests were initially administered by the Eastern Region, a foothold which it retained in the west for a number of years.

An insight into the vast volume of traffic carried by British Railways in Lancashire can be gleaned from the fact that in September 1950 they had no less than 1,897 steam locomotives based within the county. The stock consisted of 1,548 engines either formerly owned by the LMS or manufactured to their patterns by BR, 289 locomotives with a LNER lineage and sixty Riddles ex-War Department 'Austerity' 2-8-0s. They were dispersed between thirty-six motive power depots (sheds), Newton Heath and Gorton, both in Manchester, being the largest with allocations totalling 167 and 166 engines respectively. At the other end of the spectrum were Lower Ince (Wigan) with just twelve engines and Bacup with thirteen. Furthermore, locomotives from a vast array of other sheds could be seen within the county on a daily basis, some from as far away as London in the south and Glasgow in the north.

Towards the end of the decade, in March 1959, thirty-two BR steam sheds were still in use in Lancashire with a total allocation of 1,577 locomotives. Although many of the older engines had been replaced by more modern types, including eighty-three built by BR themselves to their standard designs, a surprising number of veterans were still active. Remarkably, listed amongst the ranks of the 1,259 engines from the LMS stable were seventy-five with a L&YR ancestry, fifty-four of which had been constructed during the nineteenth century, the elder statesman being 0-6-0ST No. 51336 at Fleetwood shed which had started life as an 0-6-0 tender engine back in July 1877. The 109 ex-LNER locomotives included seventy-three with a Great Central Railway parentage. The remaining 126 were ex-WD 'Austerity' 2-8-0s. Also worthy of mention is the fact that Horwich Works still maintained five former L&YR 0-6-0STs, originally built as 0-6-0s between June 1877 and June 1880, for internal shunting duties. These five were not part of BR capital stock.

During the 1960s the rate at which steam locomotives were withdrawn from service rapidly gained momentum, not only because of an increasing reliance on diesel and electric power, but also due to the closure of various lines and the loss of some traffic to the road haulage industry. Even so, in April 1965 808 steam engines remained extant at twenty-two sheds situated within the borders of Lancashire, the total being made up of 661 former

LMS types, 113 BR Standards and thirty-four ex-WD 2-8-0s. It will be noted that by this time all the ex-LNER engines had departed from the scene except for an occasional visit from across the Pennines.

By the start of 1967 it was evident that Lancashire would be one of the last outposts of steam on BR, for in January of that year fourteen sheds in the 'Red Rose County' still hosted a total of no less than 590 steam locomotives – 484 of seven different classes built to LMS drawings and 106 BR Standards of five classes. Most dominant were the Stanier 'Black 5' 4-6-0s (233 examples) and his 8F 2-8-0s (197), while the most prominent of the BR Standards were the class 5 4-6-0s (52) and the 9F 2-10-0s (32). They were employed on a variety of freight and parcels turns along with a little passenger work.

One year later, at the start of January 1968, ten Lancashire sheds were among the thirteen still open for steam on the whole of BR. The ten in question maintained a total of 310 locomotives, including 136 'Black 5' 4-6-0s and 116 8F 2-8-0s, together with six Ivatt class 4 2-6-0s (all based at Lostock Hall) and fifty-two BR Standards. The latter comprised twenty-three class 5 4-6-0s, ten class 4 4-6-0s (all at Carnforth), eighteen class 9F 2-10-0s, together with the sole-surviving Britannia Pacific No. 70013 'Oliver Cromwell' which was transferred from Carlisle (Kingmoor) shed to Carnforth at the turn of the year with a view to its use on special workings.

By May the end for steam really was in sight, with only six sheds on BR, all in Lancashire, retaining any steam duties. At the end of June the shed disposal staff at Bolton, Newton Heath and Patricroft, dropped the fires of their engines for the final time, leaving the depots at Carnforth, Lostock Hall (Preston), and Rose Grove (Burnley) as the last bastions of BR steam.

Right: It was in 1959 that British Railways started to sell off its surplus steam locomotives to private scrap merchants for breaking up, and during the ensuing years literally thousands of engines were disposed of in this way. In 1960 the Central Wagon Co. Ltd at Ince, Wigan, became involved in the work, and as well as numerous local examples they also took delivery of engines from the Eastern and Western Regions, some arriving from as far away as East Anglia and South Wales. The only Coronation class 4-6-2 to meet its doom in the Lancashire yard was No. 46243 'City of Lancaster', an engine which in past times regularly had charge of some of the crack expresses running between London Euston and Glasgow Central, such as 'The Royal Scot' and 'The Caledonian', as they threaded their way through the county along the West Coast Main Line. The Pacific is seen awaiting its fate, along with Stanier class 5MT 2-6-0 No. 42952, on 1 July 1965. Appropriately, the smokebox number plate from No. 46243, together with one of the nameplates, are now displayed in the Lancaster City Museum.

Left: At Garstang on Friday, 26 July 1968, at the end of the penultimate week of regular steam on British Railways, Lostock Hall driver Tony Gillett is seen oiling the motion of Stanier 'Black 5' 4-6-0 No. 45407, before he returned it to Preston with a local trip freight. No. 45407 is one of eighteen 'Black 5s' which were eventually preserved. Its home base is now the East Lancashire Railway at Bury, although it often spends time away working specials on the main line, particularly during the summer months.

These three sheds were then able to call on just ninety-one steam locomotives, the rest having been withdrawn.

Just over a month later, on Saturday 3 August 1968, the last rites were enacted as far as ordinary services were concerned. That day BR Standard class 4 No. 75019 headed what proved to be the final freight, a lengthy train of vans from Heysham to Carnforth, while over at Rose Grove the last Copy Pit banker, class 8F No. 48278, made its melancholy way back to the shed. That evening Lostock Hall shed had the doubtful honour of providing the power for the last two steam-hauled passenger trains, 'Black 5' No. 45212 for the 20.50 Preston to Blackpool South service and sister engine No. 45318 for the 21.25 from Preston to Liverpool Exchange. Both trains were crammed with expectant enthusiasts savouring the last moments of steam.

Next day, by way of commemoration, six enthusiasts' specials plied various routes around Lancashire, while the final farewell tour was organised for the following Sunday, 11 August. Appropriately, the valedictory special started at Liverpool Lime Street and traced the route of the erstwhile Liverpool & Manchester Railway before continuing from Manchester to Carlisle via Blackburn and Settle. On the day, 'Oliver Cromwell' and three 'Black 5s' were used on this out and back excursion. After this a few isolated collieries and other industrial establishments continued to use steam locomotives for a number of years before the railway preservation movement was left to carry the banner for steam. Today, within the old county boundary, former BR steam locomotives can be regularly seen hard at work on the revived East Lancashire Railway between Heywood, Bury and Rawtenstall and – although for administrative purposes now part of Cumbria – on the Lakeside & Haverthwaite Railway, near the southern tip of Lake Windermere, as well as at the head of the occasional main line special. However, it must be said, after August 1968 life was never quite the same again!

On a personal note I was born and bred a Lancastrian, my interest in BR steam being kindled during the mid-1950s. Thereafter, I took a very close interest in its fortunes until its demise in the summer of 1968; indeed, I was one of scores of passengers who made that fateful journey from Preston to Liverpool Exchange behind 'Black 5' No. 45318 on 3 August 1968, the last night of ordinary everyday steam. For those of us who were privileged to witness first-hand the run-down of steam it was an unforgettable era. It was, too, in the main, a very friendly environment, a period when most officials seemed to have a relaxed attitude towards shed visits, and lineside photographic permits could be obtained for the cost of a stamped addressed envelope – I had 25 miles of track at my disposal and other sections on a temporary basis. Further, I was often welcomed by signalmen into their box, a few of whom I visited on a regular basis during the late 1960s, while one or two enginemen were not averse to allowing the occasional footplate trip. By design, this volume can provide only a mere snapshot of BR steam in its last years of regular use in Lancashire, but I trust just a little of the atmosphere that prevailed at that time will shine through the following pages.

The requirements of Liverpool Exchange Station, along with some of the nearby dock lines, were looked after by the former L&YR shed at Bank Hall. Viewed from the turntable on 7 September 1965 are two of the three-cylinder Jubilee class 4-6-0s allocated to the depot, No. 45721 'Impregnable', and, furthest away from the camera in front of the four-road No. 1 shed, No. 45684 'Jutland'. On the far right can be seen the concrete coaling plant erected during the 1930s, and on the left is the west wall of the eight-road No. 2 shed. That afternoon sixteen steam locomotives, including the depot's other two Jubilees, No. 45627 'Sierra Leone' and long-standing resident No. 45698 'Mars', along with three diesels, were 'on shed'. The shed closed on 24 October 1966.

Aintree shed, in the northern suburbs of Liverpool, was opened by the L&YR in 1886, the engines based at the depot being employed almost exclusively on the movement of freight. Standing over the ash pits, after returning from a day's work on 7 September 1965, are LMS class 3F 0-6-0T No. 47289 and Stanier 8F 2-8-0 No. 48363. When the coaling plant was installed in 1937 the old coaling stage along with the large water tank on top, seen here behind No. 47289, were left *in situ*. Notice, too, the number of fire-irons, shovels etc., simply left lying around on the ground – a far cry from present-day health and safety requirements! After the shed closed on 12 June 1967 the shell of the main building remained standing for over twenty-eight years, although in an increasingly derelict condition, before demolition work began in February 1996.

The line between Liverpool Exchange and Aintree was electrified by the L&YR in 1906, with the live third-rail being extended to Ormskirk in 1913, although any trains from Liverpool which travelled beyond Ormskirk continued to be steam-hauled. On the same afternoon as the two previous photographs, with the rails and platforms glistening during a heavy downpour, BR Standard Class 4 4-6-0 No. 75049 prepares to make a brief call at Aintree with a Liverpool Exchange to Preston service. Built at Swindon in 1953, No. 75049 spent over ten years on the books of Bank Hall shed before being withdrawn from there in October 1966. Aintree is perhaps best known as the home of the famed Grand National steeplechase and at one time on race days, in addition to the numerous local services, the station was kept busy dealing with a host of excursions which arrived from various parts of the United Kingdom. After depositing their stock in the nearby marshalling yards, the engines were then made ready for their return journeys at Aintree shed, the visitors often including representatives of some of the more illustrious classes such as Patriots, Royal Scots and Britannias, which otherwise were very rarely seen at this depot. Steam was last used on the Grand National specials on 8 April 1967, the year rank outsider Foinavon took the honours in the 'Big Race' after taking advantage of the almost farcical mix-up at the twenty-third fence which blighted the chances of many of the faster horses.

On the south side of Liverpool, on former LNWR tracks, Stanier 'Black 5' 4-6-0 No. 45441 slowly rumbles through Allerton Station with a northbound train of tank wagons on 5 September 1966. Speke Junction shed, the home of No. 45441, was just a ten minute walk from this station. The overhead catenary was energised at 25kV AC in 1962, whereupon electric traction began to operate between Liverpool Lime Street and Crewe and later through to London Euston. The spur to the left of the 'Black 5' is the ex-Cheshire Lines Committee connection to their Liverpool Central to Manchester route which dives under the LNWR line just to the south of the station. Steam working on the south side of the city persisted until May 1968 when the iron horse was banished from the sheds at Speke Junction and Edge Hill, the latter once housing some of the most prestigious LMS classes of motive power such as the Princess Royal 4-6-2s, and the Royal Scot and Jubilee 4-6-0s for use on the express trains working out of Liverpool Lime Street.

Earlestown Station is situated roughly midway along the route of the historic Liverpool & Manchester Railway, some 6 miles east of Rainhill, the scene of the famed locomotive trials of October 1829 which were won by Stephenson's 'Rocket'. In due course a triangular junction was created at Earlestown with platforms on all three sides, the southern arm providing a link to the West Coast Main Line at Winwick Junction, 1 mile to the south. On 23 June 1968, with an admiring audience in attendance and Earlestown No. 4 signal box in the background, BR Standard class 5 4-6-0 No. 73069 stands on the west curve while waiting to take over the Locomotive Club of Great Britain-sponsored 'Two Cities Limited' excursion, which made two return trips between Liverpool and Manchester utilising various routes. No. 73069 relieved Stanier class 8F 2-8-0 No. 48033 when the special arrived from the Manchester direction a few minutes later. No. 73069 was the last of the Standard class 5s built between 1951 and 1957 to remain in traffic, not running its last until August 1968.

Opposite: Carlisle (Upperby)-based Britannia Pacific No. 70032 'Tennyson' storms past Winwick Junction on the West Coast Main Line on 20 August 1966. It is about to take the divergence towards Wigan with a northbound parcels train. At first the fifty-five members of the Britannia class, introduced between 1951 and 1954, were scattered far and wide throughout BR, but eventually, in the 1960s, they all ended up on the London Midland Region and became a very familiar sight throughout Lancashire. When new in December 1952, No. 70032 was sent to Holyhead shed, but during the following month it was reallocated to Longsight shed in Manchester where it was assigned to diagrams which mainly covered the Manchester London Road (now Piccadilly) to London Euston expresses. 'Tennyson' stayed at Longsight until February 1960 when it was moved across Manchester to Trafford Park shed, before being transferred to the capital and attached to Willesden shed in January 1961. It was withdrawn in September 1967 after spending its last three years at Carlisle, having had spells at both Kingmoor and Upperby sheds.

Just to the north of Warrington a rather unkempt BR Standard class 5 4-6-0 No. 73137 drifts south past Dallam Branch Sidings signal box with an up mixed freight on 24 August 1966. No. 73137 was one of thirty members of this class that were fitted from new with Caprotti rotary cam poppet valve gear. The locomotive was in its final twelve months of activity and, indicative of the fact that the end was fast approaching, had already lost both its smokebox number plate and its cast 9H (Patricroft) shed plate. Access to Warrington (Dallam) shed was gained from the track on the left, the depot closing on 2 October 1967.

BR Standard class 4 4-6-0 No. 75043 bides time in the loop at Trafford Park, Manchester, as Fairburn class 4 2-6-4T No. 42113 hurries by with a local stopping service from Manchester Central on 29 June 1965. A path led from the left-hand side of the footbridge to the ex-Cheshire Lines Committee Trafford Park shed, rail access being gained from the points situated by the semaphore signals to be seen near the back of the train hauled by No. 42113. During the early days of BR the shed was home to a variety of former LNER and LMS classes, but by the 1960s any engines which in pre-nationalisation days had been owned by the former company had either been transferred elsewhere or taken out of service. On the far left of the photograph is the main stand of Manchester United's Old Trafford football ground, and to its right is the platform used in connection with matches at the stadium. This was the era when the likes of George Best, Bobby Charlton, Denis Law and Nobby Stiles were donning the famous red jersey and in the season just ended United had again qualified for the European Cup, having finished as champions of the old First Division.

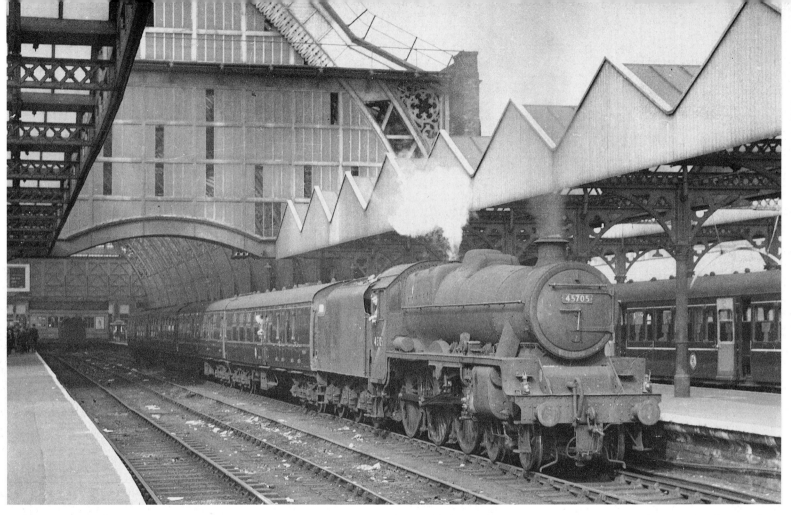

Reminiscent of the days at Manchester Central when Jubilee class 4-6-0s held sway on trains to London St Pancras, No. 45705 'Seahorse' pulls away from this former Cheshire Lines Committee terminal with the much less demanding four-coach 17.22 to Buxton on 29 June 1965. During the summer of 1965 'Seahorse' was regularly rostered to this train, whereupon it then stayed overnight at Buxton in order to work the next morning's 08.00 commuter service from the spa town back to the city. The station closed on 5 May 1969, after which it was used as a car park for a number of years before the area within the 210 foot single-span train shed, a listed building, was revamped and reopened as the G-Mex Centre in 1986. As such it has proved an ideal venue for staging exhibitions, concerts and sporting events, although to this day the atmosphere within its cavernous interior still retains a distinct whiff of steam!

Amidst the grime-encrusted surroundings of the ex-L&YR Manchester Victoria Station, 'Black 5' 4-6-0 No. 45420, built for the LMS by Armstrong Whitworth of Newcastle-upon-Tyne in 1937, has its tender replenished from the column at the east end of platform 17 on 30 March 1968. When much of the station was rebuilt in 1995, this portion was redeveloped as part of the 19,500-seat Nynex (now the MEN) arena with direct access provided from the new platforms.

Two Ivatt class 2 2-6-0s exchange greetings at Manchester Victoria on 23 August 1966. On the right No. 46505 stands in the 'Wallside' siding, used by banking engines waiting to assist eastbound trains climbing away from the station, while No. 46437 gathers speed with the District Engineers inspection saloon a few moments after departing from the far end of platform 11 on the left. Both engines were constructed by BR, No. 46437 at Crewe in 1950 and No. 46505 at Swindon in 1952. The tender of a third engine, at the west end of platform 12, is visible to the right of No. 46437. The station's present-day four through platforms, largely enclosed by the concourse to the arena, occupy the area shown here.

For many years much of the newsprint industry was concentrated in Manchester and every night a number of trains were despatched from the city laden with the next morning's papers. In fact, people all over the north of England, North Wales, and parts of Scotland, were once highly dependent on the efficiency of this operation if they were to catch up with all the latest happenings over breakfast. Here, during the early evening of 29 July 1967, BR Standard class 5 4-6-0 No. 73045, on one of its last duties before withdrawal the following month, has just brought a lengthy set of newspaper vans from Red Bank Sidings into Victoria's platform 11 ready for loading. This particular platform was linked to Manchester Exchange Station's platform 3. It stretched for 2,194 feet and was the longest on BR.

Most of the former LNWR Manchester Exchange Station (actually located in the city of Salford) was protected from the elements by a splendid triple-arched overall roof. Idling time in a short bay at the west end, while on duty as the station pilot on 30 March 1968, is Caprotti valve gear-fitted BR Standard class 5 4-6-0 No. 73128. Notice that the numerals on the side of the cab, and the British Railways crest on the tender, have been highlighted rather amateurishly. The locomotive was a product of Derby Works in August 1956 and was withdrawn from Patricroft shed in May 1968 after less than twelve years service. The station itself was closed twelve months later on 5 May 1969, whereupon all trains on the north side of Manchester used Victoria, as had been the case prior to the opening of Exchange in June 1884.

For a number of years steam and diesel locomotives were uneasy companions at many BR sheds, the newcomers preferring a much more sanitised environment to the filthy smoke-ridden atmosphere that was experienced at the steam sheds. Here, at the former LNWR shed at Patricroft, near Manchester, two Stanier class 8F 2-8-0s (the one on the right is No. 48170) share the facilities with three Brush Type 2 diesel-electric locomotives on 15 June 1968. Within two months of this date diesel and electric power would have total command of BR's day-to-day traction requirements, with the few remaining steam locomotives all having been taken out of service.

On a crisp 10 December 1960, BR Standard class 4 4-6-0 No. 75048 catches the afternoon sun as it departs from Bolton Trinity Street with a train for Rochdale. In October 1953 the newly-built No. 75048 was despatched from Swindon Works to Accrington shed, before being attached to Bank Hall from November 1955 until April 1966. It was destined to be among the last steam locomotives in service on BR, being withdrawn from Carnforth shed in August 1968.

Against a backdrop of the parish church of St Peter, LMS 'Black 5' 4-6-0 No. 45156, minus its 'Ayrshire Yeomanry' nameplates, begins the gruelling 7-mile climb from Bolton to Sough Summit while *en route* towards Blackburn with the 'GC Enterprises' excursion from Stockport to Carnforth on 4 August 1968. This was one of six enthusiasts' specials which trekked around Lancashire on this particular Sunday to mark the end of steam traction on BR. For most of its life No. 45156 was based in Scotland – hence its name. It was transferred south from St Rollox shed in Glasgow to Newton Heath in April 1957, after which Lancashire became its adopted county until its fire was extinguished for the last time at the conclusion of this excursion.

To enable engines fitted with the necessary scoop to top up their tenders or side tanks while on the move, ten sets of water troughs were laid around Lancashire, seven by the L&YR and three by the LNWR. Here, on a bitterly cold January day in 1965, a BR Standard class 4 4-6-0 approaches the troughs installed by the L&YR at Lostock, to the west of Bolton, with a three-coach local service bound for Wigan. The end of the troughs, between the up fast and slow lines, can be seen at the bottom right-hand corner of the picture.

During the late 1880s the L&YR established its main workshop facilities at Horwich, near Bolton, and starting in 1889 a total of 1,840 steam locomotives (including five 1ft 6in. gauge engines for its own internal rail system) were constructed at the factory, the last being BR Standard class 4 2-6-0 No. 76099 in 1957. The smallest locomotives built at Horwich (excepting the narrow gauge examples) were the Aspinall-designed L&YR class 21 0-4-0STs for shunting dock areas and other yards which demanded the use of short-wheelbased engines. Often referred to as 'pugs' they weighed only 21 tons 5cwt, fifty-seven of the class leaving the works between 1891 and 1910. No. 51218 started life in 1901 as L&YR No. 68 and in its later years was to spend much of its time away from its native heath, eventually migrating to South Wales during the early 1960s. In 1963 it returned to Horwich for an overhaul, and looking resplendent after a spell in the erecting shop, was posed in the works yard on 15 June 1963. It was withdrawn from Neath shed in September 1964 as the last remaining 'Lanky' engine on BR. Fortunately, it still survives and is now normally based on the Keighley & Worth Valley Railway in West Yorkshire.

Awaiting their turn to enter the erecting shop at Horwich Works on 26 June 1960 are, from left to right, LMS class 4F 0-6-0s nos. 44593, allocated to Stoke shed (code 5D), and 44071 from Canklow, near Rotherham (41D), Stanier class 8F 2-8-0 No. 48166 from Nuneaton (2B), and BR Standard class 4 2-6-0 No. 76023 from Lancaster (Green Ayre) (24J). On the right is the tender of Stanier Mogul No. 42958 from Crewe North (5A). That day fifty-six steam locomotives were recorded during a guided tour of the works. As far as Horwich was concerned the steam era ended on 6 May 1964 when the last steam locomotive to go through the shops, Stanier 8F No. 48756, left for its home at Carlisle (Kingmoor) (12A). After this the works focused its resources on the repair and overhaul of electric multiple units and wagons, before it finally closed at the end of December 1983.

During the 1960s there were far too many sombre occasions to mark the closure of various branch lines and stations. On a rain-soaked 25 September 1965, Bolton shed provided Stanier class 4 2-6-4T No. 42626 to power the last passenger train from Horwich, the 12.05 SO (Saturdays only) service to Bolton. Here, adorned with a wreath along with a suitable headboard, and with a few of the 'mourners' hanging out of the windows of the leading non-corridor coach, No. 42626 prepares to stop at Lostock Junction. The engine had been specially spruced-up for the occasion, including the painted buffers and smokebox door hinges, by a group of local enthusiasts. The goods shed at Horwich was retained until the following April, whereafter the short 1-mile branch from Blackrod continued in use solely for traffic to and from Horwich Works.

Nearing the end of the 3 mile 1-in-97 climb from Hindley, Jubilee class 4-6-0 No. 45627 'Sierra Leone' blasts through Westhoughton, on the ex-L&YR route from Wigan to Bolton, with a special carrying Liverpool supporters to an FA Cup fifth round tie against Bolton Wanderers on 20 February 1965. Later in the day the Liverpool devotees returned home in triumphant mood, their team having won 1–0. During the 1950s and 1960s this was the author's local station.

Two years later, on 18 February 1967, Bolton entertained Arsenal in the fourth round of the FA Cup. Here, the empty stock of one of the three specials laid on to transport the 'Gunners' fans from London to Bolton speeds through Westhoughton behind 'Black 5' 4-6-0s Nos. 45409 and 45374 *en route* to Kirkdale Carriage Sidings, Liverpool, where the stock was serviced prior to the return journey. The steam locomotives had taken over from electric traction at Stockport. On this occasion the match ended 0–0, with Arsenal going on to win the replay at Highbury 3–0 the following Wednesday.

LMS class 4 2-6-4T No. 42474 and Jubilee class 6P 4-6-0 No. 45590 'Travancore' double-head a lengthy summer Saturday extra from the West Riding of Yorkshire to Southport along the down fast line at Hindley North on 13 July 1963. No. 42474 was shedded at Agecroft (26B) and 'Travancore' at Newton Heath (26A). The signal box at Crow Nest Junction can be discerned in the distance beyond the station platforms. At the time three routes converged at this junction, the direct lines from Manchester via Atherton (the path followed by the train depicted here) meeting those from Bolton via Westhoughton and from Blackrod (on the Bolton to Preston line). Today, only the former slow lines through Hindley (the two tracks to the right of the goods loop in the foreground) remain in use for trains running between Manchester and Wigan via either Atherton or Bolton, the route to Blackrod being closed to all traffic on 9 September 1968.

Overleaf: BR Standard class 4 4-6-0 No. 75047 bides time at the former L&YR-owned Wigan Wallgate Station while awaiting the 'right away' with a stopping service for Liverpool Exchange in May 1965. During the 1950s and 1960s the road behind the fence on the right, which gave access to the goods yard, was a favourite haunt of many railway enthusiasts in that it also offered a good view of the ex-LNWR West Coast Main Line through Wigan North Western Station.

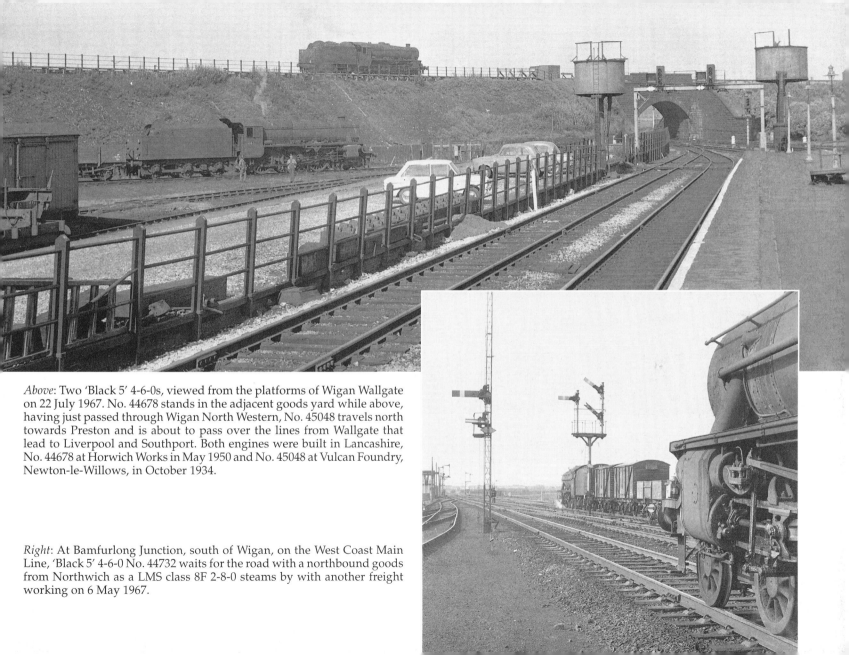

Above: Two 'Black 5' 4-6-0s, viewed from the platforms of Wigan Wallgate on 22 July 1967. No. 44678 stands in the adjacent goods yard while above, having just passed through Wigan North Western, No. 45048 travels north towards Preston and is about to pass over the lines from Wallgate that lead to Liverpool and Southport. Both engines were built in Lancashire, No. 44678 at Horwich Works in May 1950 and No. 45048 at Vulcan Foundry, Newton-le-Willows, in October 1934.

Right: At Bamfurlong Junction, south of Wigan, on the West Coast Main Line, 'Black 5' 4-6-0 No. 44732 waits for the road with a northbound goods from Northwich as a LMS class 8F 2-8-0 steams by with another freight working on 6 May 1967.

During the 1960s the occasional brake van tour afforded those who were not averse to travelling in Spartan conditions an opportunity to sample various secondary routes. Here the 'Wigan Area Brake Van Tour' approaches Lower Ince, on the former Great Central line from Glazebrook to Wigan Central, behind Stanier class 5 Mogul No. 42968 on 13 August 1966. Normal passenger services along the route had been concluded in November 1964. The wagons straddling the bridge behind the brake vans are on the Springs Branch, which joined the West Coast Main Line by Springs Branch shed. Since its inception this branch had only been used by freight trains and in its heyday served a number of local collieries and other industrial concerns, although by 1966 it only went as far as the Central Wagon Works (see page 4). The line at the higher level passing over the two bridges ran between Hindley and Pemberton, and was constructed by the L&YR to enable expresses between Manchester Victoria and Liverpool Exchange, as well as goods traffic, to bypass Wigan Wallgate Station. All the lines depicted here have long since been closed. However, No. 42968 is still extant, the only member of this once forty-strong class so favoured. Today, it is resident on the Severn Valley Railway at Bridgnorth, Shropshire.

The engine shed at Springs Branch, situated just over a mile to the south of Wigan North Western Station, was once owned by the LNWR and eventually covered sixteen roads. In September 1950 the shed had a complement of fifty-seven locomotives. Eighteen months later, in March 1952, the nearby ex-GCR shed at Lower Ince was closed and its stock of thirteen class J10 0-6-0s and one LMS class 2 Mogul, No. 46428, transferred to Springs Branch. Similarly, when the former L&YR Wigan depot was abandoned in April 1964, most of its allocation was moved across the town to Springs Branch. One year later, in April 1965, the shed still had fifty-eight locomotives on its register. In the first of two pictures taken at the shed, fuel is being discharged from the rather distinctive coaling plant into the tender of Ivatt class 2 2-6-0 No. 46515 on 29 June 1966. The engine was built at Swindon at the end of 1952 and spent the first thirteen years of its life working over the former Cambrian lines from Oswestry shed in Shropshire, before moving to Speke Junction in January 1965. It was relocated to Springs Branch in May 1966, before being withdrawn from the shed twelve months later.

LMS class 4F 0-6-0 No. 44490 and Stanier class 5 2-6-0 No. 42963 repose in the yard on 6 September 1965. Both engines were based at Springs Branch although No. 44490 had just been withdrawn from service. That afternoon fifty-seven steam locomotives of twelve different classes were sighted, either on shed or passing along the adjacent main line. All were common to the area except for an ex-Great Western Railway 5700 class 0-6-0PT, No. 9753, formerly of Tyseley shed (Birmingham), which was among a small batch of engines waiting to be towed to their final destination at the Central Wagon Works for scrapping. The shed bolted its doors to steam on 4 December 1967 but continued in use for many years thereafter for the benefit of diesel and electric locomotives. In recent times the site has been utilised by the freight company English, Welsh & Scottish Railway as a depot for the recovery and distribution of components from withdrawn diesel locomotives.

At the south end of Wigan North Western Station, water appears to be cascading everywhere as the tender of Britannia Pacific No. 70027 'Rising Star' is topped up before it continues its journey towards Crewe with a parcels train on 21 January 1967. Meanwhile, the crew seem to be pondering how they might stem the flow of water without sustaining a drenching! After its release from Crewe Works in October 1952, 'Rising Star' spent almost nine years on the books of the Western Region at Cardiff (Canton) depot, before moving to Aston (Birmingham), on the London Midland Region, in September 1961. Finally, from September 1966, after further postings during the interim to Holyhead, Crewe North, Crewe South, Llandudno Junction, and Crewe South again, the locomotive worked from Carlisle (Kingmoor) shed prior to being withdrawn in June 1967.

Overleaf: LMS class 8F 2-8-0 No. 48081 clatters through Wigan North Western with a rake of empty coal wagons from Whitebirk Power Station, Blackburn, to Bickershaw Colliery, Leigh, on 26 August 1967. Of the 852 members of this class built between 1935 and 1946, including many for the Ministry of Supply, 194 were put together in Lancashire, sixty-nine by Vulcan Foundry at Newton-le-Willows, fifty by Beyer Peacock & Co. Ltd of Manchester and seventy-five in the LMS workshops at Horwich. No. 48081 was completed by Vulcan Foundry in January 1937. The line from Manchester to Wigan Wallgate descends beneath the footbridge on the far right-hand side of the print. During the summer of 1967 the station certainly looked in need of some refurbishment with much of the roof missing from the platform canopies. Notice, too, the leaking water column at the platform end in front of the goods hoist, along with the brazier which does not appear to have been cleaned out after use the previous winter. The long-overdue improvements were carried out a few years later, when the station was completely rebuilt in preparation for the inauguration of the overhead electrification scheme which enabled electric locomotives to continue north from Weaver Junction, south of Warrington, through to Glasgow Central from 1974.

At Euxton Junction the former L&YR line from Bolton merges with the ex-LNWR route from Wigan. Viewed trundling south from Euxton Junction towards Wigan on 4 September 1967 is BR class 9F 2-10-0 No. 92102 with a heavy load of anhydrite from the mines at Long Meg, north of Appleby, *en route* to the ICI plant at Widnes. Euxton Junction signal box is on the left, while the signals in respect of trains using the tracks to and from Bolton, hidden by the embankment on the right, can be seen above the third and ninth hoppers. No. 92102 first saw the light of day at Crewe Works in August 1956. Two months after this photograph was taken, and like so many other steam locomotives built in the 1950s, it was prematurely condemned when but a mere eleven years old.

During the steam age a vast acreage of land was set aside for holding and marshalling freight wagons. Here, on 2 July 1966, roaring past the sidings at Farington Junction, on the climb from Preston, is Britannia class 7P 4-6-2 No. 70042 'Lord Roberts' with the eleven-coach 13.46 Barrow to Euston service. At Crewe an electric locomotive took over from the Pacific for the remainder of the journey to London. The tracks diverging to the right behind the signal box lead to Blackburn. The coaling plant at Lostock Hall engine shed was just out of sight to the right of the electricity pylon. After completion at Crewe Works in April 1953 'Lord Roberts' was employed by the Eastern Region from Stratford shed in London until May 1958, when it transferred its allegiance to the London Midland Region. It was marked for the cutter's torch in May 1967 after spending the final seventeen months of its life based at Carlisle (Kingmoor) shed.

The eight-road Lostock Hall shed, commissioned by the L&YR in 1882, was conveniently situated alongside the station of the same name. In 1937 the efficiency of the depot was much improved by the installation of an ash disposal facility and a coaling plant. Later, in September 1961, when the ex-LNWR Preston shed was closed, many of its engines were relocated to Lostock Hall. Although at the beginning of January 1968 the sands of time were rapidly running out for the iron horse, the shed foreman at Lostock Hall still had twenty-nine steam locomotives at his disposal, namely six Ivatt class 4 2-6-0s, eighteen Stanier 'Black 5' 4-6-0s and five Stanier class 8F 2-8-0s. Viewed from the doorway at the back of the shed during the evening of 10 February 1968 is 8F No. 48077 with its Lostock Hall 10D shed plate clearly visible. On the adjacent road is another 8F, an Ivatt class 4 and a 'Black 5', while on the right the shed breakdown crane stands ready in case of need. It appears that one of the employees at the shed was determined to park his car as near as possible to his place of work! The shed officially closed to steam on 5 August 1968 but was in use again the following weekend when the engines entrusted to haul the final BR commemorative steam special from Liverpool to Carlisle and back were prepared here.

A few minutes after negotiating Preston Station southbound, Scottish Region BR Standard class 5 4-6-0 No. 73100 cautiously pulls a Dundee to Blackpool train round the now-closed sharp curve from Todd Lane Junction to Lostock Hall Junction and joins the line from Blackburn on Saturday 9 July 1966. Shortly afterwards the train passed Lostock Hall shed before leaving the Liverpool line at Engine Shed Junction so as to regain the West Coast Main Line at Farington Curve Junction. From there it proceeded in a northerly direction before threading Preston Station for a second time in about fifteen minutes or so, before it veered off towards the Fylde Coast at Maudlands Junction. This 5-mile detour, which obviated the need to reverse at Preston, was a path regularly taken on summer Saturdays by a host of specials from the north to Blackpool, the start of the Glasgow Fair holiday usually being a particularly noteworthy day in this respect. As regards No. 73100, during its entire working life, which lasted from August 1955 until January 1967, it was based at Corkerhill shed in Glasgow. Thus, on the day in question and this far south of the Scottish border, it was a very welcome and noteworthy visitor to Lancashire.

Stanier class 8F 2-8-0 No. 48167 ensures that anyone 'at home' in the properties on the left is well aware of its presence as it blasts through Huncoat Station, near Accrington, with a rake of empty coal wagons returning from Fleetwood Wyre Dock to Burnley on 7 May 1968. On the right are the former Huncoat Colliery exchange sidings, the pit having wound its last coal three months earlier on 9 February 1968. No. 48167, a Rose Grove engine, remained at work until the shed closed at the very end of steam on 5 August 1968.

On its way south from Preston with an up express, Britannia Pacific No. 70033 'Charles Dickens' pounds past the site of the former station at Farington (last used in March 1960) on 9 July 1966. Prominent on the skyline is the slender 309 foot high spire of St Walburge's Roman Catholic church by Maudlands Junction, to the north of Preston Station. A minute or so after the photograph on page 36 had been taken, No. 73100 would have crossed over the West Coast Main Line by the bridge seen here above the fifth carriage, before starting the descent from Engine Shed Junction, just off the picture to the left, to Farington Curve Junction.

Workaday steam in Lancashire. Fairburn class 4 2-6-4T No. 42224 travels south along the up slow line at Farington with the three-coach 16.22 Preston to Wigan stopping train on 2 July 1966.

At Farington Curve Junction Carnforth-allocated 'Black 5' 4-6-0 No. 44874 surges from beneath Bee Lane bridge on the up fast with a train for Manchester on 12 August 1967. Services destined for Liverpool (now cut back to Ormskirk) or Blackburn, accessed these routes by way of the points seen in the foreground on the slow lines. As will be noted from the position of the signal box, close by the bridge beyond the near arch, the signalman had a very restricted view of any approaching northbound trains.

During the Second World War R.A. Riddles designed an easy to maintain yet powerful 2-8-0 locomotive for the Ministry of Supply. Between 1943 and 1945 no less than 935 were put together, 390 in Lancashire by Vulcan Foundry at Newton-le-Willows, with the North British Locomotive Company in Glasgow being responsible for the rest. All but three of these rather ungainly machines saw service overseas, many never returning to their homeland after the war ended. Eventually 733 of their number became the property of British Railways and here No. 90556 (former War Department No. 77090 built by Vulcan Foundry in 1943) slowly clanks through the former East Lancashire Railway portion of Preston Station as it heads south in the direction of Todd Lane Junction with a long link of empty coal wagons on 5 March 1960. This was a typical duty for the class.

The station pilot at Preston, Ivatt class 4 2-6-0 No. 43088, pauses awhile during the early evening of 25 November 1967. Seventy-five of this class were completed at Horwich Works between 1947 and 1952, although No. 43088 was one of those built at Darlington in 1950. It only arrived at Lostock Hall shed in August 1967 and was withdrawn at the end of the year. The one member of the class to have been preserved, another former Lostock Hall inhabitant, No. 43106, is now maintained by the Severn Valley Railway at Bridgnorth, Shropshire.

At one time on summer Saturdays and Bank Holidays the rails from Preston to the Fylde Coast would be chock-a-block with seasonal extras. Trains destined for Blackpool Central, either via St Anne's or the direct Marton line, went their separate ways at Kirkham North Junction, while those bound for Blackpool North or Fleetwood continued along the same metals as far as Poulton-le-Fylde, where they too parted company. By 1968 it was a different story, with Blackpool Central and the main station at Fleetwood having been abandoned and the number of specials drastically reduced, although steam still retained a presence. Here, on 6 May 1968, Rose Grove-based class 8F 2-8-0 No. 48730, built at Darlington for the LNER in 1945, but handed over to the LMS before nationalisation, leaves Poulton-le-Fylde for Preston with a mixed freight. The long island platform at Poulton Station can be seen beyond the signal box on the right.

On Saturday 20 April 1968 the Railway Correspondence and Travel Society sponsored the 'Lancastrian No. 2 Rail Tour'. The excursion started from Liverpool Lime Street and, after visiting Fleetwood Wyre Dock, was hauled to Windermere by the last remaining Britannia Pacific in traffic, No. 70013 'Oliver Cromwell', which had been retained specifically for such occasions. Here, No. 70013 makes a spirited exit from Preston past Maudlands Junction while *en route* to the Lake District. The train reporting number – 1T85 – was unusually positioned just above the buffer beam rather than on the smokebox door. The Fylde Coast lines are on the right, the Pacific having travelled over this route a little earlier on its way into Preston from Fleetwood, before following the circuitous route via Lostock Hall around the southern fringes of the town (now a city). The ex-LNWR Preston shed (closed in September 1961) occupied the area to the far right of the picture, beyond the coast lines.

Carlisle (Kingmoor)-allocated BR Standard class 9F 2-10-0 No. 92071 confidently climbs the 1-mile 1-in-98 bank from Lancaster Castle Station with an up freight on 22 July 1967. At the side of the down line, just beyond the chequered board by the GPO staff hut, can be seen the mailbag exchange apparatus, whereby bags hung from the side of passing Travelling Post Office trains could be deposited at speed into the netting after it had been outstretched towards the track. Similarly, trains could collect sacks suspended from the adjacent post once the arm had been swung round through 180 degrees. Some fifty yards or so nearer Lancaster a second post for this purpose can be discerned behind a further warning board. This is yet another once-common facet of the railway industry that has been consigned to history.

Opposite inset: 'Black 5' 4-6-0 No. 44758 arrives at Lancaster Castle with the summer dated 17.45 Windermere to Blackpool service on 31 July 1967. The faded lettering on the buffer beam of No. 44758 denotes it was previously allocated to Lancaster (Green Ayre) shed, the engine moving to Carnforth (10A) when Green Ayre closed in April 1966. The oil tanks standing on the through road on the left were headed by class 8F 2-8-0 No. 48247.

Opposite main: On 15 July 1967, framed by the semaphore signals at the north end of Lancaster Castle Station, 'Black 5' 4-6-0 No. 45415 passes on the up through line with a southbound fitted freight. The signals were controlled from the partly obscured Lancaster No. 4 signal box on the left. On the right is the connection to the former Midland Railway Lancaster Green Ayre Station which was electrified using overhead wires energised at 6,600V AC back in 1908. The line was closed to passengers on 6 January 1966, although some of the electrification masts are still in position.

REFRESHMENTS

44758

It is only at Hest Bank, between Lancaster and Carnforth, that trains travelling the entire length of the West Coast Main Line from London to Glasgow actually come within sight of the sea. While looking across Morecambe Bay towards the Lake District, 'Black 5' 4-6-0 No. 45092 was photographed propelling a mixed assortment of stock towards the station after collecting a couple of wagons from the goods yard on 3 August 1967. The train is on the single line that leads to Bare Lane and Morecambe. The up and down tracks of the West Coast Main Line are in the foreground.

On the same day as the upper picture, during its last weeks of activity before being withdrawn the following month, No. 70010 'Owen Glendower' runs northbound tender-first through Hest Bank with a couple of parcels vans in tow – a rather menial task for a class 7 Pacific! The locomotive's cast nameplates, formerly affixed to the smoke deflectors, had been replaced by hand-painted versions, with the English spelling on one side and the Welsh 'Owain Glyndwr' on the other. The junction points for the Morecambe branch are just off the platform end, the popular seaside resort being visible in the distance to the right of the locomotive. Looking back to 1967, some might well ask what better place was there to spend a week's holiday than in one of the camping coaches stabled in the goods yard?

A member of the most powerful class, and the largest numerically, introduced by British Railways, Carlisle (Kingmoor)-based 9F 2-10-0 No. 92012 stands at the up platform at Carnforth after bringing a set of empty coaches through the Westmorland fells from Carlisle on 31 July 1967. The first of this class, which eventually totalled 251, emerged from Crewe Works in January 1954 and the last, the celebrated No. 92220 'Evening Star', from Swindon Works in March 1960. It was not until June 1958 that any became permanently based in Lancashire when five were moved to Newton Heath. By 1965 the total had increased to forty-one, with Speke Junction and Warrington (Dallam) sheds then having an allocation as well as Newton Heath. At the start of 1968 eighteen 9Fs remained in Lancashire, ten at Speke Junction and eight at Carnforth, the last three in service, Nos. 92077, 92160 and 92167, being withdrawn from the latter shed in June 1968. Carnforth Station, which was used as the location for scenes in the 1945 film classic *Brief Encounter*, has recently been renovated, although today it is only possible to travel to Lancaster from the platforms serving the Barrow and Leeds lines, which are to the left of the photographer.

Motive power in transition. Looking north from the footbridge to the south of Carnforth Station on the same day as the previous picture, 8F 2-8-0 No. 48158 and 'Black 5' 4-6-0 No. 44826 prepare to haul a train of oil tanks from Heysham across the Pennines to Leeds via the 'Little North Western' route, as Brush Type 4 diesel-electric locomotive No. D1625 (later renumbered 47044, then 47567) hurries south with an up Anglo–Scottish express. In the background, at the station, a diesel multiple unit forming a service from Barrow awaits a suitable path to proceed south, while another three-car DMU is stabled behind the steam locomotives. On the far right is Carnforth No. 2 Junction signal box. Above No. 44826 can be seen the ash disposal plant and coaling tower at the six-road Carnforth shed. Opened in 1944, in order to consolidate the work previously undertaken at the old Furness, LNWR and Midland Railway sheds at Carnforth, it normally had an allocation of about forty locomotives, although the figure had increased to fifty-five by the start of 1967 after the closure of Lancaster (Green Ayre) shed the previous year. Twelve months later, in January 1968, the numbers had decreased to thirty-nine, the stock consisting of twenty LMS 'Black 5s' and nineteen BR Standards, ten class 4 4-6-0s, eight 9F 2-10-0s, and Britannia 4-6-2 No. 70013 'Oliver Cromwell'. The shed was utilised by steam until 3 August 1968, the last day of steam on normal everyday services on BR. Carnforth shed is now owned by the West Coast Railway Company and, while it is no longer open to the public, it still houses a number of preserved steam locomotives, some of which can be seen from time to time on the main line system.